All About Advertising

Carmel Reilly

Contents

All About Advertising

What Is Advertising?

Advertising is a type of communication that is used to **promote** and sell products and **services**.

Advertising comes in the form of advertisements, or ads. Ads for products are everywhere. They can be found in online media and on TV, radio and **billboards**, as well as in newspapers and magazines. Ads are usually produced by **advertising agencies** on behalf of businesses wanting to sell their **goods**. Advertising agencies are part of a worldwide, multibillion-dollar advertising industry.

Ads are all around us in our everyday lives.

Advertising has a huge effect on our lives today. For example, in the USA, the average person could see thousands of ads a day. Studies from the USA also show that children could see up to 40 000 ads a year. While advertising informs people about products and services, it also has its downsides. Advertising only focuses on the positive aspects of a product, rather than giving a balanced view. Ads can also encourage people to buy goods that they do not need or that are unhealthy for them.

Some ads take up large amounts of space in newspapers, so that it's impossible to ignore them.

Children and young people can come across thousands of ads every day, particularly if they use smartphones.

The History of Advertising

Advertising has existed for as long as there have been goods to sell. However, as the number of products has grown, so has the amount of advertising.

From Ancient Times to the 1800s

In ancient Greece and China, **merchants** made signs and painted pictures on city and town walls to help sell their goods. In medieval times, **town criers** announced products and services along with the latest news.

This ancient sign from Turkey advertised which goods a shop sold.

Town criers often carried bells so they could get people's attention.

However, it was not until the **Industrial Revolution** that advertising became important. From the late 1700s onwards, the amount of manufactured goods rose quickly. This gave people more choice about what they could buy. But with so many options for sale, manufacturers needed to make sure their products stood out. The best way to do this was to advertise.

During the Industrial Revolution, stores in the USA were filled with lots of products for people to choose from.

The Industrial Revolution also brought many social changes. People became wealthier, more people learnt to read and write and many travelled for work. As a result, companies began placing ads in popular newspapers and magazines. Companies also made billboards and put posters up to grab people's attention as they went out and about.

Technology Changes Everything

In the twentieth century, radio and TV provided new ways to advertise. Ads were no longer made up of only printed words and pictures. Suddenly, companies could speak to people directly in their homes through ads shown during breaks between programs. Advertisers also **sponsored** programs and created "infomercials", which are ads that seem like a normal TV program. By the late twentieth century, some TV channels *only* showed advertising. Many of these channels ran 24 hours a day.

A TV show host films a commercial for jam in the middle of a TV program in the 1950s.

In the 1990s, large numbers of people began to use computers and go online. The internet became home to new types of advertising, such as **banner ads**, pop-up ads and video ads that played on websites. Around the same time, the video game industry started making "advergames", a form of advertising that features a product within a video game.

In the early 2000s, people began to use smartphones. The **apps** on smartphones gave people easier access to **social media** sites, which began to show ads scattered throughout their users' **feeds**. Today, social media sites often feature **influencers** promoting products.

cute_cupcakes

Rosanna Pansino, a famous influencer on YouTube, attends an event at a bakery as a form of advertising.

Creating Advertising

Since the twentieth century, most ads and **advertising campaigns** have been created by advertising agencies.

Advertising Agencies

Advertising agencies are companies run by people who create and manage advertising for businesses wanting to sell their products.

In the 1800s, the first advertising agents were people who sold print space in newspapers for ads. However, as the number of products for sale grew, the role of advertising changed. Agents started to learn what helped to sell different products, and some of them began creating their own ads on behalf of companies, instead of only selling ad space.

Newspapers were widely read in the 1800s, so they were the perfect place for advertising.

As time went on, advertising agencies started to do more than just make ads. By the mid-twentieth century, agencies were running whole advertising campaigns, doing market research, and planning and buying ad space. Advertising agencies had become the experts.

Today, advertising is a vast industry. Advertising worldwide is worth hundreds of billions of dollars.

Advertising Campaigns

Advertising campaigns are ways to make people aware of a company, brand or product. They usually include showing a range of ads across different media and developing **branding**, which includes the logo and product design.

The "got milk?" advertising campaign was created to sell more milk in the USA in the 1990s.

How Ads Work

The aim of advertising is to alert a target audience to a product and convince them that they want it. Advertisers can do this in two ways. The first is through the content of an ad, or what is presented. The second is through the placement and timing of the ad, or where and when it is shown.

Target Audience

A target audience is the group of people who are most likely to buy a product.

Content

The content of ads can vary a lot depending on the products and their target audiences. Even products that are quite similar might be advertised differently. Breakfast cereals are a good example of this.

People in advertising agencies work hard to determine the best way to reach different target audiences.

Ads for some brands of cereal focus on the health benefits. They might highlight the amount of fibre or vitamins the cereal contains. These ads are usually aimed at the parents of children and teenagers.

However, many cereal ads focus on the fun side of eating the product. They are full of colour and movement, and the video ads have catchy music that grabs the viewer's attention. These kinds of ads are aimed at children. While children do not usually buy cereal themselves, they can influence what their parents buy.

Cheerlos cereal used hearts in their advertising to show that eating their cereal was part of a healthy diet.

This cereal ad from 1954 was designed to look like a picture book in order to grab children's attention.

Placement and Timing

The target audience for an ad also affects where and when it appears. For example, when ads for cereals are shown on **streaming services** or internet sites, they are usually played before or during programs that are watched by families and children. This is because families with children are the target audience for cereals. The same ads might be shown on TV after school or around breakfast time during children's programs.

Ads for cereals can also be seen on billboards, on public transport and around transport hubs. This is so they can be seen by parents and children as they travel to work and to school. Athletes and other celebrities also sometimes promote cereal products on their websites or social media, where parents and children who follow them will see the promotion.

Olympic cyclist Chris Hoy appeared in an ad for a breakfast cereal to help sell it.

This ad for a luxury perfume featuring the glamorous actor Nicole Kidman has been placed on a street with expensive shops in Paris, France.

On the other hand, ads for luxury goods such as jewellery and expensive cars are shown in different ways, because they are aimed at adults. Some of the places these ads are found include fashion magazines, electronic billboards in city centres and on certain websites and social media feeds. Luxury products are also often featured by social media influencers on their pages.

The World Reflected in Advertising

Advertising is often criticised for not **reflecting** the real world. Some people say ads fail to represent everyone equally and that they do not show some groups in a balanced way.

Who Is Seen, and How Are They Seen?

Many countries are home to a wide range of cultural groups. In places such as Australia and Aotearoa New Zealand, more than a quarter of the population is born overseas, and a lot of people speak languages other than English at home. Advertising is starting to reflect a more diverse population than it did a few years ago. However, there are still groups that are not well represented, such as First Nations peoples or people with disabilities.

A company that makes shaving products held a campaign to show a more diverse range of people in their ads.

In advertising, women have traditionally been shown as **homemakers**, while men are shown as wage earners and decision-makers. Today, many women work in jobs and workplaces that women didn't have access to before. Nonetheless, women are still seen in ads for kitchen, bathroom and laundry products more often than men. Studies also show that, overall, men appear and speak more often in ads than women.

Although this ad from the 1950s is for a type of cabinet, the main focus is a woman making breakfast in the kitchen.

This ad from 2007 shows a woman and child promoting laundry detergent.

Truth in Advertising

There are laws against telling outright lies in an ad. However, ads do not always tell the whole truth. The aim of ads is to create a want or a need. They do this by showing something in a perfect way so that viewers might want it for themselves. For example, a face cream ad in a magazine might show a model with beautiful skin. The ad suggests to readers that they, too, will have beautiful skin if they use the same face cream. What readers might not know is that the image has been altered to make the model's skin appear perfect.

Looking at ads that have altered images can have a negative effect on how we view ourselves.

Greenwashing

Concern for the environment in recent years has led to something known as "greenwashing". Greenwashing occurs when companies that might not have environmentally friendly practices look for ways to show that they are doing good for the environment. For example, a mining company that is responsible for polluting a nearby river might advertise that it has planted trees. Planting trees has some benefit to the environment, but it would not change the fact that the river is still being polluted.

Some ads feature images with lots of green colours, so that the audience thinks that the company and its products are environmentally friendly.

How Advertising Influences People

Advertising changes the way people see the world. Ads can make certain products and services more desirable, or they can make some brands appear better than others. Ads can create stories that viewers want to be a part of, for example, by showing families or friends enjoying a product together. People remember ads when the ads tap into their emotions by making them laugh, feel sad or sometimes cringe. However, ads can also encourage unrealistic ideals about how people should look or act, and they can promote unhealthy behaviours such as gambling or eating junk food.

This ad for Coca-Cola doesn't show the product prominently. Instead, it focuses on a family spending time together, to convince viewers to buy the product.

Ads Everywhere

Whether people are on the street, at home or online, they are almost constantly surrounded by advertising. It is estimated that some people see up to 10 000 ads a day. One study of viewers who watch TV and online videos showed that they were watching twice as many ads as they thought they were watching. People are also constantly exposed to branding – that is, the logos and designs associated with well-known companies or products. For this reason, certain brands of clothing, mobile phones, computers and fast food are easily recognisable.

Some brands are seen so often that we can recognise them instantly, such as the logos for different types of cars.

It's All About You

In the twenty-first century, ads became more **personalised**, or aimed at individuals. Internet **search engines** can now collect **data**, or information, every time a person visits a website, watches a video or clicks on an ad. People's locations and the places they regularly visit can also be tracked through smartphone apps, such as ones that use maps. This information is then used to target people with ads about products related to the places they have visited online and in the real world.

Computer and smartphone users are constantly exposed to ads on websites and social media sites. Many people click on them to find out more details. However, they do not always realise that these ads are tailor-made for them.

The things we buy can influence the type of ads we see online.

The information that is collected on computers and smartphones is sold to data collection companies. These companies use the data to look at any trends, such as which products people are searching for. Advertisers are able to buy this information to help them work out who the target audiences should be for certain products and how best to reach them.

Data collection companies use information to help advertisers target different audiences.

The ads we see on our smartphones have often been chosen for us depending on what we've clicked on in the past.

Not-for-Profit Ads

Advertising can also be used to influence people for a good cause. Sometimes, not-for-profit organisations and government agencies use advertising to inform people about important issues or campaigns. These kinds of ads might include messages on public health matters, campaigns against violence or community projects and concerns. For example, during a drought, there might be an advertising campaign encouraging people to use less water. Another ad might let local citizens know about a council-run festival.

Covid-19 Messages

There have been many health messages from government agencies since 2020 about Covid-19. Some asked people to wash their hands, wear masks and keep a 1.5-metre distance from other people. Others advised people to stay at home or to get vaccinated against the virus.

Advertising campaigns during the Covid-19 pandemic helped inform people about how to slow the spread of the disease.

Advertising is also used by charities to raise awareness for their causes, promote change and encourage people to donate money. Political parties advertise as well, to alert people about their **candidates** and their key ideas in the build-up to an election, and sometimes to ask for donations.

Charities often print flyers that can be placed in people's mailboxes to advertise their cause.

Not-for-profit ads are placed in different media depending on the target audience. Charities and political parties often send messages directly to targeted people by mail, email or text. On the other hand, public health campaigns aim for their messages to reach as many people as possible. The media they use can range from apps and websites to billboards, TV and radio.

Reactions to Advertising

People react to advertising in different ways. Some people find ads annoying and try to block them wherever possible. Others dislike the way advertising encourages them to buy more than they normally do. Some parents do not like the effects of advertising on children. They try to reduce the number of ads their children see, often by limiting children's time on electronic devices.

A lot of people see so many ads that they develop ad **fatigue**. This means they simply start to ignore most ads. Because of ad fatigue, advertisers are always looking for new ways to get viewers' attention, such as advergames. Advergames can hold people's attention by actively engaging them in a video game, often rewarding them with prizes for taking part, such as discounts.

Seeing ads every day can give us ad fatigue.

Advertising has become a large part of our lives. It can be entertaining and often provides people with information about different products. However, it does not always offer the full story. The best way to approach advertising is to understand how it works and always think critically about its content.

Advertising is all around us, so it's important to know how it affects us.

Jay's Blog

Junk Food Ads for Kids Should Be Banned

This week at school, we have been talking about advertising. Advertising is all about selling things. It does this by flooding us with persuasive messages about products to convince us how great they are. Ads don't give us a balanced view or take our health into account. Worst of all, ads for unhealthy foods unfairly target children. What I've learnt makes me feel that ads for junk food should be banned from online kids' shows, streaming services and TV.

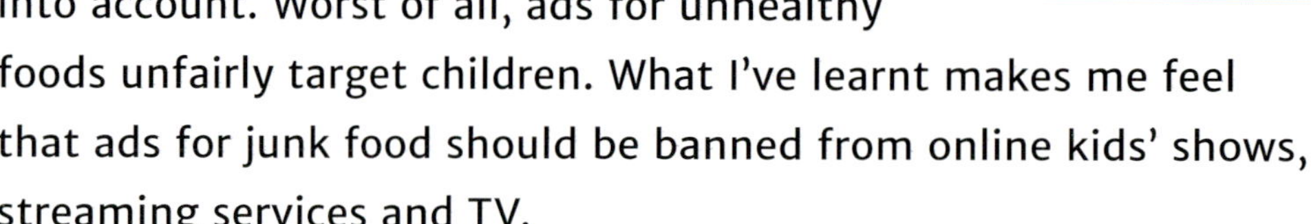

Streaming services and TV programs for kids show lots of ads for unhealthy foods.

Firstly, there are far too many junk food ads that play during kids' programs. I can understand that ads are trying to sell something. I also know junk food isn't good for me. However, I still find it hard to resist wanting junk food when I see those ads over and over again. This is especially true when I'm hungry just before dinner!

Secondly, ads only show the positive side of a product. They often focus on how great something tastes, or they might show a group of kids eating and having fun. This makes us believe that if we eat that product, we'll have fun, too. These ads never say that junk food is really not very good for us at all and can even make us sick. Ads don't tell us what a healthy diet should be.

Junk food ads often include images of kids playing sports to make the food seem healthier.

Finally, ads for junk food are mostly aimed at kids. This is unfair. Research shows that kids can spend up to 32 hours a week looking at screens. It also shows that kids under the age of five don't understand that ads are different from the programs they are watching, so they can't tell that advertisers are trying to sell them something. Even older children may not have the skills and experience to understand advertising. Persuading kids to eat junk food when they're young like this leads to lifelong bad habits and poor health.

Eating lots of junk food, such as pizza, can be an unhealthy choice, but companies don't show this in their ads.

Eating healthy foods can make kids happier and help them to build healthy habits for later in life.

I believe we should ban junk food ads on streaming services and TV, especially during programs that kids are watching. I read that junk food ads were banned on TV many years ago in Quebec, a province in Canada. Since then, people there have been spending much less money on junk food than before. I am sure a ban on ads would help keep children in this country happy and healthy, too.

Let me know what you think in the comments!

Jay

Don Joe

Love your fresh take on ads about junk food and their influence on kids!

Glossary

advertising agencies (*noun*) businesses that make and manage advertising for different companies

advertising campaigns (*noun*) organised groups of ads that sell something

apps (*noun*) applications, or programs, that are downloaded to a mobile device

banner ads (*noun*) ads along the sides, top or bottom of webpages

billboards (*noun*) large signs placed outside that ads are displayed on

branding (*noun*) the name, logo and design that a company is recognised by

candidates (*noun*) people who want to be elected to a position in a government

data (*noun*) any facts or information that can be studied

fatigue (*noun*) a feeling of not wanting something because you have experienced it so much

feeds (*noun*) webpages that show new content being added instantly

goods (*noun*) items that are bought and sold

homemakers (*noun*)	people whose main job is to take care of their house and family
Industrial Revolution (*noun*)	the time when machines began to be used to do work in Europe and the USA
influencers (*noun*)	people with many online followers who recommend different items to buy
merchants (*noun*)	people who sell things in large amounts
personalised (*adjective*)	designed for a particular person
promote (*verb*)	to try to make something popular
reflecting (*verb*)	showing an image of or representing something as it really is
search engines (*noun*)	computer programs that look for a word or phrase on the internet
services (*noun*)	tasks that are done for a customer
social media (*noun*)	websites and apps that allow users to create and share content with other users
sponsored (*verb*)	gave money to support a TV program or an event in return for advertising
streaming services (*noun*)	websites or apps that play TV shows and movies
town criers (*noun*)	people who shouted the news on the street, in the past

Index